Martin Taylor's Advanced

JAZZ**GUITAR**LICKS PHRASE**BOOK**

Over 130 Intermediate to Advanced Licks for Jazz Guitar

MARTIN**TAYLOR**
WITH JOSEPH**ALEXANDER**

FUNDAMENTAL**CHANGES**

Martin Taylor's Advanced Jazz Guitar Licks Phrase Book

Over 130 Intermediate to Advanced Licks for Jazz Guitar

ISBN: 978-1-78933-215-5

Published by **www.fundamental-changes.com**

www.fundamental-changes.com

Over 11,000 fans on Facebook: **FundamentalChangesInGuitar**

Instagram: **FundamentalChanges**

For over 350 Free Guitar Lessons with Videos Check Out

www.fundamental-changes.com

Cover Image Copyright: Lister Cumming, used with permission.

Contents

About the Authors

Dr Martin Taylor MBE is a virtuoso guitarist, composer, educator and musical innovator.

Acoustic Guitar magazine has called him, "THE acoustic guitarist of his generation." Chet Atkins said that Martin is, "One of the greatest and most impressive guitarists in the world," and Pat Metheny commented that, "Martin Taylor is one of the most awesome solo guitar players in the history of the instrument."

Widely considered to be the world's foremost exponent of solo jazz and fingerstyle guitar playing, Martin possesses an inimitable style that has earned him global acclaim from fellow musicians, fans and critics alike. He dazzles audiences with a signature style which artfully combines his virtuosity, emotion and humour with a strong, engaging stage presence.

Martin has enjoyed a remarkable musical career spanning five decades, with more than 100 recordings to his credit. Completely self-taught, beginning at the early age of 4, he has pioneered a unique way of approaching solo jazz guitar that he now breaks down into seven distinct stages in order to teach others.

Joseph Alexander is one of the most prolific writers of modern guitar tuition methods.

He has sold over 600,000 books that have educated and inspired a generation of upcoming musicians. His uncomplicated tuition style is based around breaking down the barriers between theory and performance, and making music accessible to all.

Educated at London's Guitar Institute and Leeds College of Music, where he earned a degree in Jazz Studies, Joseph has taught thousands of students and written over 40 books on playing the guitar.

He is the managing director of *Fundamental Changes Ltd.*, a publishing company whose sole purpose is to create the highest quality music tuition books and pay excellent royalties to writers and musicians.

Fundamental Changes has published over 120 music tuition books and is currently accepting submissions from prospective authors and teachers of all instruments. Get in touch via **webcontact@fundamental-changes. com** if you'd like to work with us on a project.

Introduction from Martin

Hi and welcome to my *Advanced Jazz Guitar Licks Phrase Book.*

I want to begin by asking you a question. If you were to visit another country and needed to communicate in another language, would it be more useful to be given a dictionary or a phrase book?

Of course, that's an easy answer. If you don't even know the words you need, how on earth would you find them in a dictionary? However, given a phrase book, you can immediately copy the sounds and begin to communicate. As you gradually learn more phrases from your book and copy the sounds that people are making, you'll start to combine them and suddenly you're beginning to speak.

The quickest way to learn to communicate in a new language is always to learn some phrases and copy the sounds that native speakers make. You won't reach for the dictionary or use a "theory of language" grammar book, you'll just directly copy some language you've heard and apply it in a real-life situation.

This is why it continues to astonish me that people treat learning the language of jazz guitar any differently. I've had students approach me who know far more theory than me – all the clever scales and arpeggios they *could* use on this or that chord – but when they actually play the guitar, more often than not their solos just don't sound jazzy. Guitarists are often guilty of taking a "theory first" approach to learning jazz because they've been told that jazz is "hard" or "all about the theory". The reality is, playing jazz is much simpler than you might think. Often, the great players we idolise are playing fairly simple ideas, just with great time and phrasing.

How did they develop this phrasing? By copying and playing the language of the musicians *they* admired.

This book is all about learning the language of jazz guitar, and you're going to do this by listening to me play some of my favourite phrases. Having learnt them, you'll incorporate them into your own playing. You'll copy my notes, phrasing and rhythms. You'll learn hundreds of pieces of *vocabulary*. You'll begin to combine these into sentences that will grow to form solos. As you do this, you'll begin to understand how the language of jazz soloing sounds and *feels*.

You may be thinking, "But what about the *theory!*" My answer to that is, you didn't learn to speak with a book of grammar in your hand, you copied the adults around you. Maybe some theory came a little later when you were at school and you learnt about adjectives and verbs and iambic pentameter, but I'm sure you were doing a wonderful job of speaking before you were introduced to these complex ideas.

In this book, there is no theory! There's just language, phrases and the vocabulary that forms the basis of the rich jazz language. I made a conscious decision *not* to include lick breakdowns because I want you to focus solely on the communication and *voice* of your music.

These phrases are organised so that you can use them over very common chord progressions in jazz. The popular chord sequences that occur in most jazz standards are here. Don't worry if you spot a sequence I've not covered – this book isn't supposed to be an exhaustive list of licks you can play in every possible situation. Once you've learned to speak, you will quickly be able to apply the phrasing and language to any chord sequence you like.

Have fun!

Martin Taylor

August 2020

A Note from Joseph

This is the second of Martin's Jazz Guitar lick phrase books. This time the material is aimed at intermediate to advanced players who want to refine and grow their jazz vocabulary. For those readers who bought the previous volume, the material here represents a step up in difficulty. However, the format is identical, and the licks are played over the same musical progressions as before – so you are in familiar territory!

Writing and recording these books has been a complete pleasure from start to finish. It's not every day you get to go into the studio with one of your musical heroes and ask them to demonstrate all of their licks. As Martin has mentioned, this book was conceived as a phrase book for guitarists looking to learn the language of jazz soloing and when we set about gathering the material, it seemed the easiest thing to do was to ask Martin to use a pedal to loop some common jazz sequences, hit record on the camera, and let him play for 20 minutes.

The beauty of this approach was that we could see how Martin took a small seed of an idea and let it grow throughout a solo. When he felt that idea had blossomed, he took a few bars break and began with a different seed. It really hit home how the greatest jazz solos are built from tiny, yet powerful pieces of vocabulary that combine to tell a story which gradually unfolds throughout the choruses – and Martin is certainly one of the greatest jazz storytellers in the world. He talks about his process in more detail in his previous book *Single Note Soloing for Jazz Guitar*.

We spent a day in the studio drinking coffee and recording, and in fact we gathered enough material for several books. This book is the intermediate-advanced edition and we previously released a beginner level book. Martin also recorded a whole load of longer solos and soon these will become a book of jazz guitar etudes. These will teach you how to organically develop a musical idea throughout a solo – another idea Martin covers in depth in *Single Note Soloing for Jazz Guitar*.

Once the recording was done, we cut the long videos into individual licks and sent them off to the annoyingly talented Levi Clay for transcription. He worked his magic and we could begin assembling the book.

Martin has requested that we tread very lightly on the theory when it comes to these phrases because he wants you to focus on sound, phrasing and developing the language – just as you did when learning to speak as a child. There's no need to over-think these ideas. If it helps to reassure you, most of Martin's playing is based on a diatonic foundation and tension is created by "filling the gaps" with chromatic passing notes, rather than by applying complex theoretical ideas.

We've organised this book into language that fits over several common sequences, so not only will you learn to recognise these progressions by ear when they occur in music, you'll have an idea of the type of vocabulary that works in that situation. However, there's a much broader point here that I want you to think about.

In language, the same words and sentences will work in an almost infinite number of contexts, and once you understand how the words work you can use them almost anywhere. You can make conversation with almost anyone who speaks your language, even if they're from a massively different background or location. The language of jazz soloing is no different. Once you understand the vocabulary you can adapt it to any new chord sequence.

Rarely do we get such direct insight into the language of a true jazz guitar master. Learn it, then go and make it your own.

Joseph

How to Use This book

When you open a traditional language phrase book, you'll see that the phrases are organised into "situations". The opening section might address greetings, the next might look at ordering food in a restaurant, which could be followed by directions to famous landmarks, and so on…

This jazz soloing phrase book is organised into situations too, but our situations are the chord sequences you'll solo over in common jazz standards.

We've taken eight common chord sequences and taught you some essential vocabulary for each. However, just as with spoken language, the vocabulary you use to greet someone on the street can also be used in a restaurant or shop. In other words, phrases learnt for one musical situation are often appropriate in other contexts too.

After learning your first few sentences, you'll begin to pick up on the natural patterns, pronunciation and grammar of the language, so it gets quicker and quicker to learn new phrases and speak with authority.

In this book, you'll learn the perfect vocabulary for the following chord sequence "situations":

- Major to minor II V Is

- Minor ii V i

- I vi ii V turnarounds

- Dominant 7 chords moving in 5ths

- Static dominant 7 chords

- II V sequences descending in semitones

- Static minor 7th chords

- The minor blues

These chord sequences form the backbone of hundreds of jazz standards and by learning phrases for each one you'll quickly learn to "speak jazz" authentically. As these ideas naturally combine and get rooted into your subconscious, they'll quickly begin to influence the sound of the phrases you create yourself when improvising.

To use this book effectively, try to spot the chord sequences listed above when they occur in tunes you're working on. If you're working on a song with a lot of II V Is, you could begin in Chapter One. If you're working on a rhythm changes (I vi ii V) tune like *I Got Rhythm* or *Oleo*, you could begin with Chapter Three.

Next, *audition* the phrases in that chapter by listening to the audio examples. If there's one that really jumps out at you and you think it matches your current ability, that's the one you should learn first. It jumped out at you for a reason.

Just like our spoken language, we often reuse phrases that resonated with us when we first heard them. If you only *learn* phrases you like, you will only *play* phrases you like. Well, most of the time!

By being selective about which phrases you learn and repeat, you can control the musical language that you internalise, which will become the source material for your own creativity.

When you sit down to learn a phrase, make a commitment to yourself to memorise it. To play anything fluently it needs to become a part of you.

To memorise a line, break it up into small rhythmic chunks of just a few beats and repeat each chunk until you can't get it wrong. Then move on to the next chunk or section and repeat the process. Next, combine the first two sections and play them until they're fluent before adding the third, and so on. Remember, you're not just learning a lick, you're programming yourself with how the language feels.

Once you've memorised a line, you should start using it in an actual solo as soon as possible. To begin with, try to play it perfectly at the appropriate point in the tune. After a while, your musical brain will start to want to vary the phrase. Don't fight this! These phrases are just a starting point for you. The idea is to teach you the language so you can form your own unique sentences.

As you gradually add more and more phrases to your vocabulary, they'll combine and evolve to create your own voice on the guitar.

Get the Audio

The audio files for this book are available to download for free from **www.fundamental-changes.com.** The link is in the top right-hand corner. Click on the "Guitar" link then simply select this book title from the drop-down menu and follow the instructions to get the audio.

We recommend that you download the files directly to your computer, not to your tablet, and extract them there before adding them to your media library. You can then put them onto your tablet, iPod or burn them to CD. On the download page there are instructions and we also provide technical support via the contact form.

For over 350 free guitar lessons with videos check out:

www.fundamental-changes.com

Over 11,000 fans on Facebook: **FundamentalChangesInGuitar**

Tag us for a share on Instagram: **FundamentalChanges**

Chapter One – Major II V I to Minor II V I

In most jazz guitar lick books, you'll often find isolated ideas that are difficult to get your head around without a clear frame of reference, but I wanted to teach you phrases in a more musical context. When you learn licks in isolation, there is a tendency for your solos to become disjointed. You'll finish one idea. Then. Think about the next. Then play it. Before stopping… Just like the previous few sentences!

Jazz isn't like that. The lines flow like water across the chord changes. So, if you want to create a beautiful flow, you need to think beyond the phrase you're playing at that moment.

In this chapter you'll learn phrases that span a loop of the famous jazz standard *Autumn Leaves*. It begins with a Major ii V I IV (Am7 – D7 – GMaj7 – Cmaj7) and moves into a minor ii V i (F#m7b5 – B7 – Em). It's a great sequence to play over to master major and minor ii V Is.

Because I'm *not* going to give you a breakdown of every single line, I want you to audition the phrases using the audio tracks and start by learning the ones you like. However, I do want to pass on some guiding principles about the ideas I used to create these phrases. Think of these as tools you can use to build your own phrases in the future. Knowing which tools I used to create the phrases, and listening to *how* I used them, will give you a clear insight into how to compose your own phrases.

Varying phrases. Often I will take a seed of an idea and develop it. It might be a simple phrase that I play once, then play again with some variation, then vary again, etc. Connecting strong phrases helps to tell a story with your solo. But development doesn't only have to be taking a simple idea and gradually making it more complex, you can also do it by developing strong rhythmic patterns. For example, you can play a phrase, then play it again, but vary the rhythm, or vary which beat of the bar it falls on. Look out for phrase "themes" and rhythmic variation in all of the licks that follow.

Focus on tonal centres. Often when I look at a complex set of chord changes, I'll immediately distil it down into broad tonal centres. From this simple beginning you can get more complex if you want to. Taking each chord at face value and trying to play a phrase that perfectly encompasses its sound is hard work and, ultimately, quite unmusical. More often than not, you'll be overthinking the harmony and forgetting to play a memorable phrase.

In Example 1b, to begin with I've chosen to focus on the A minor sound of the opening bars, and I'm using notes from the A Melodic Minor scale to describe that sound. When the progression shifts into the minor ii V I in bar five, I focus on the tonal centre on E minor, and my phrases are drawn from E Melodic Minor. Breaking things down like this helps to keep the focus on the music more than the changes.

Target notes. Still with simplicity in mind, I'll often play a phrase with just one a target note in mind. Over the A minor chord in bar one, I might focus on the 9th (high E string, seventh fret) to create an Am9 sound. Over the D7 chord in bar two, my target might be the b9 (an Eb note on the B string, fourth fret) to create a D7b9 sound. I think of these target notes simply as *colours* that create a particular sound. I'm still not overthinking the changes – I'm just thinking about what colours in my harmonic palette I'd like to highlight.

Chromatic passing notes. Following on from the last principle, when I have a target note in mind, I'll often use chromatic passing notes (notes that don't belong to the chord I'm playing over) to reach my destination. In bar five of Example 1f, you'll see a clear example of this. I want to target the 3rd of the B7 chord (a D#) in bar six, and I use a long chromatic run to target that note, which starts in the previous bar. Passing notes are a great way to give your lines momentum and a sense of "arrival" when you hit the target.

Don't forget to breath! If we want to communicate clearly, we need to leave gaps between our phrases when we speak. When people speak in very long sentences without pausing for breath, it's hard to process that information, and the same is true in jazz. Saxophone and trumpet players have to take a breath between playing streams of notes, so there are natural pauses and clear phrases in their playing. Because guitarists don't need to take a breath, it's easy to overplay, so it's important to remember to take "breaths". In Example 1f , even though I play a couple of long phrases, these are broken up with several breaths. As a result the longer lines can be understood and the whole line doesn't sound cluttered.

Finally, a word about learning the phrases…

Study one line at a time and initially focus on the individual phrases that make up the whole. Play along with the audio until you can match the feel. When you're confident, work on the next few notes and repeat the process until you can play the whole line fluently.

Also find backing tracks in new keys and play the vocabulary in different parts of the fretboard. The goal is to completely internalise one idea before moving on to the next. When you have learned three or four phrases, something wonderful will happen: they'll begin to combine as you improvise over the backing track and will gradually evolve into your own unique language.

When you apply this language to new tunes you'll find that you'll immediately have something to say on any ii V sequences you come across. The bigger picture is that the understanding of the language you've developed here will help you to quickly play authentic-sounding jazz ideas on *any* section of the tune, almost by ear. The more vocabulary you learn, the more you'll have to say.

Here are some important standards you should know that contain Major ii V Is. There are hundreds, but this quick list should get you started. There will be a list of relevant tunes at the end of each section.

Important jazz standards that contain Major II V I chord sequences

- *All the Things You Are*

- *Autumn Leaves*

- *Here's That Rainy Day*

- *Line for Lyons*

- *The Nearness of You*

Before you start learning the following ideas, remember to audition them using the audio tracks and start with the one that jumps out at you. If you've not downloaded the audio already, you can get it from **www. fundamental-changes.com**.

Without further ado, here is a selection of ii V jazz guitar phrases for your enjoyment.

Example 1a:

Example 1b:

Example 1c:

Example 1d:

Example 1e:

Example 1f:

Example 1g:

Example 1h:

Example 1i:

Example 1j:

Example 1k:

Example 1l:

Example 1m:

Example 1n:

Example 1o:

Example 1p:

Example 1q:

Example 1r:

Example 1s:

Example 1t:

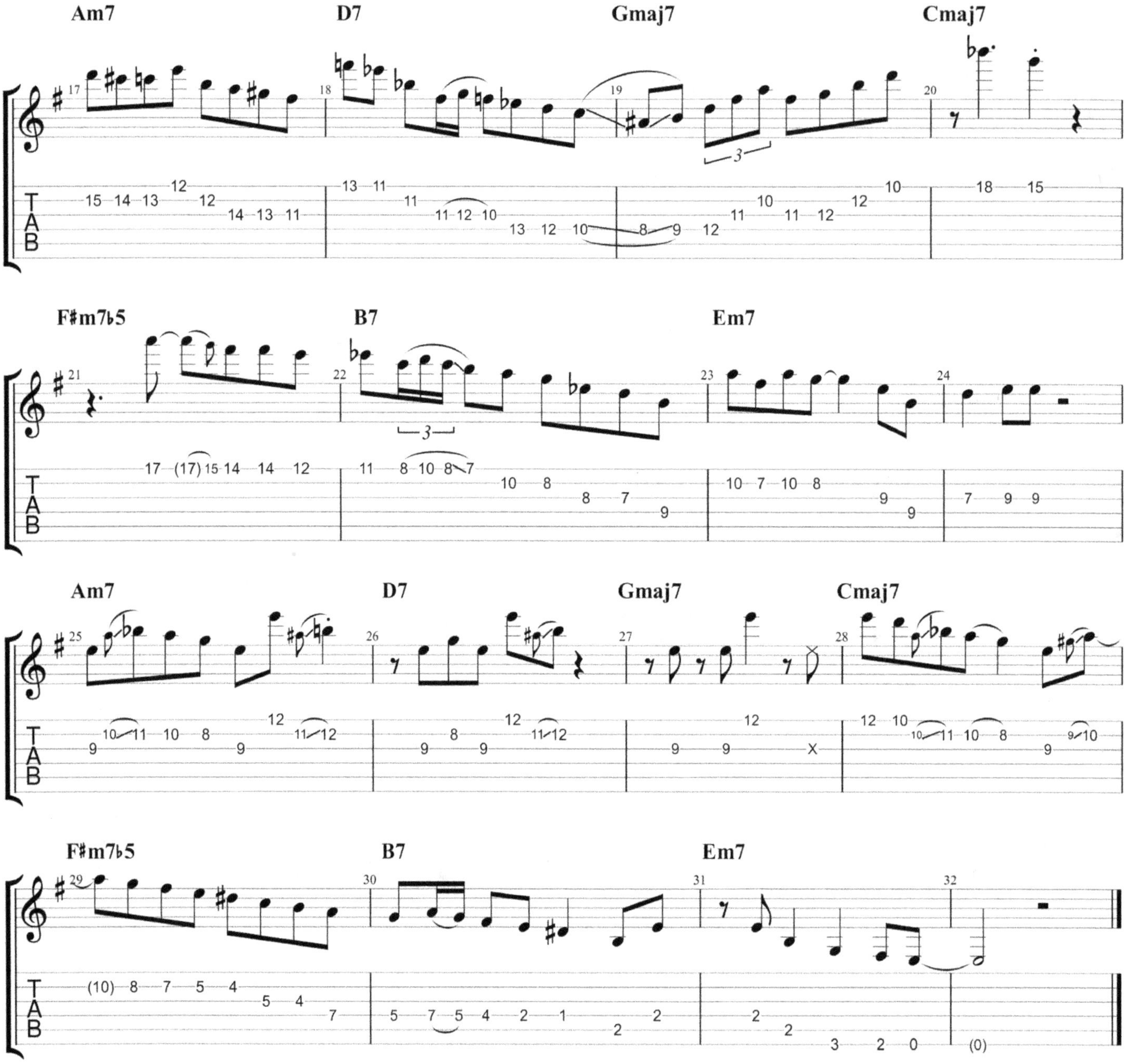
Am7
D7
Gmaj7
Cmaj7
F#m7♭5
B7
Em7
Am7
D7
Gmaj7
Cmaj7
F#m7♭5
B7
Em7

Example 1u:

Example 1v:

Example 1w:

Chapter Two – Minor II V I

The minor ii V is another extremely important sequence to master in jazz, and occurs almost as often as its Major ii V cousin. In the previous chapter you mastered many phrases that began on a Major ii V and flowed into the minor ii V. This means that each minor ii V phrase grew organically out of the Major ii V phrase and was strongly related to the original idea.

In this chapter I wanted to focus on the minor ii V exclusively and add some important new vocabulary to your phrase book, since there are plenty of minor key jazz standards and Latin tunes that use this sequence.

The phrases are mostly diatonic and based around the appropriate scales and arpeggios, but again I add chromaticism to create surprise and tension. I also make use of rhythmic variation to create well-defined, memorable phrases. Look at bars 5-8 of Example 2c and you'll see how a fairly simple phrase can be made to stand out by playing a strong rhythmic pattern. In this example I chose to play triplet phrases that *rub* against the 4/4 beat.

A productive practice idea is to copy a tiny part of the phrase which has a strong rhythm that you connect with. Try to keep playing that rhythm for as long as you can over the chord sequence. It's a powerful way to break out of the habit of playing regular 1/8th notes. Often guitarists assume that jazz soloing is just endless streams of 1/8th notes, but if you look at the notation below, you'll see it's anything but!

Audition these phrases by playing the audio examples first and begin by learning the one that most jumps out at you. Learn it by practicing in time with the audio, then play it by yourself against a backing track before moving on to the next one. When you have memorised it, move on to the next one. I suggest learning just two or three phrases before using a backing track to combine them with some of the ideas in the previous section.

When you're ready, try learning a new minor ii V tune from the list below, so that you apply your vocabulary in a musical setting.

Important jazz standards that contain minor ii V i chord sequences

- *Alone Together*

- *Autumn Leaves*

- *Beautiful Love*

- *How Deep is the Ocean?*

- *Softly, as in a Morning Sunrise*

Example 2a:

Example 2b:

Example 2c:

Example 2d:

Example 2e:

Example 2f:

Example 2g:

Example 2h:

Example 2i:

Example 2j:

Example 2k

Example 2l

Example 2m

Example 2n

Example 2o

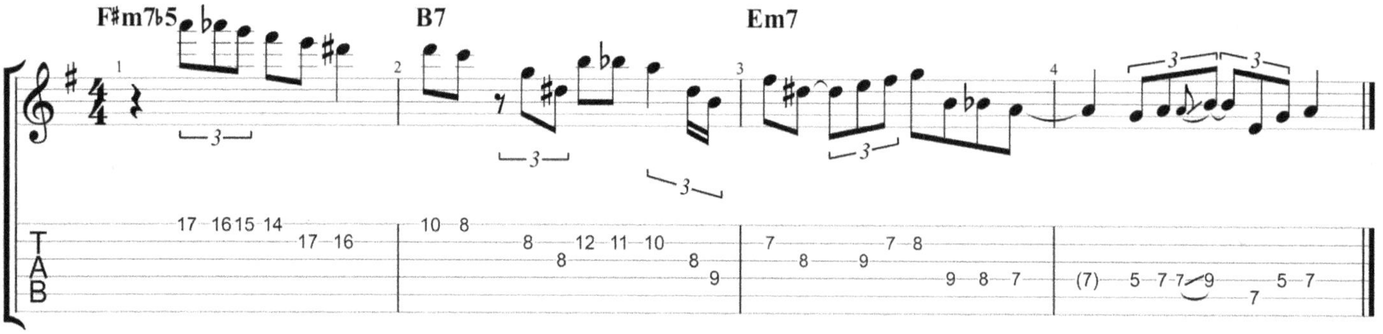

Chapter Three – I vi ii V Bb Slow

The I vi ii V chord sequence is the backbone of any "Rhythm Changes" tune, such as *I Got Rhythm* and *Oleo*. It is included here in its *diatonic* form (where all the chords naturally occur in the key) but you'll also see it played as variations, where all chords are dominant (I7 VI7 II7 V7), or with all the chords dominant except for the ii (I7 VI7 iim7 V7).

The following phrases are all played in the key of Bb Major (BbMaj7 – G7 – Cm7 – F7) as this is the most common key for rhythm changes, but it'd be useful for you to learn them in the key of G Major too.

The phrases in this chapter are played over a slower than usual tempo for Rhythm Changes. Many of the contrafact tunes written using this sequence are played very quickly, but here we are getting used to the shape of the changes. It's always good to slow down a fast-moving sequence to really understand the "geography" of the harmony and understand where it's leading. In Chapter Four I'll show you a collection of phrases at a faster tempo.

Here, you'll find lots of 1/8 note phrases, which are easier to play at this tempo. Use this opportunity to really focus on making the phrases swing and sit in the pocket of the groove. Pack as much expression as you can into each phrase.

Also listen to a few versions of the following important Rhythm Changes tunes.

Important jazz standards that contain I vi ii V chord sequences

- *I Got Rhythm*

- *Oleo*

- *Anthropology*

- *The Flintstones*

- *Moose the Mooche*

Example 3a:

Example 3b:

Example 3c:

Example 3d:

Example 3e:

Example 3f:

Example 3g:

Example 3h:

Example 3i:

Example 3j:

Example 3k:

Example 3l:

Example 3m:

Chapter Four – I vi ii V Bb Fast

In this chapter the phrases are played over a more up tempo I vi ii V sequence. Most of the lines here are still composed from 1/8 note phrases, but when playing at a brisker tempo it becomes even more important to leave breaths, so you'll notice plenty of short rests that break up the phrases.

Rhythm also becomes more important at a faster tempo. It's tempting to play long streams of 1/8 notes, but punchy rhythmic phrases will make more of an impact. Example 4b is a case in point. After four bars of playing phrases closely linked to the changes, it's time for something different, so in bars 6-7 a simple two-note repeating phrase provides the contrast.

Notice too, in bars 3-5 of Example 4c, how the line is composed of short phrases punctuated by quick breaths. It makes the whole line sound far less predictable.

Here are a few more Rhythm Changes tunes for you to explore.

Important jazz standards that contain I vi ii V chord sequences

- *Dexterity*

- *Rhythm-a-ning*

- *Lester Leaps In*

- *Steeplechase*

- *The Eternal Triangle*

Example 4a:

Example 4b:

Example 4c:

Example 4d:

Example 4e:

Example 4f:

Example 4g:

Example 4h:

Example 4i:

Example 4j:

Example 4k:

Chapter Five – Dominant Cycle of 5ths Slow

The bridge section of most Rhythm Changes tunes (see previous two chapter) is formed from a cycle of dominant 7 chords that move in fifths.

In the key of Bb Major, this is most commonly played as D7 – G7 – C7 – F7.

I've included soloing phrases for this section for a few reasons. First of all, it nicely rounds off the previous chapters, as now you have vocabulary for the whole tune. Secondly, cycles of fifths pop up in a number of jazz standards which aren't Rhythm Changes, so it's an important movement to get used to – even if the chord qualities aren't always dominant 7. Also, this is a good opportunity to learn language that fits over a dominant chord that doesn't immediately resolve to a major 7 or minor 7 in the next bar.

In this chapter we'll tackle the cycle of fifths at a slower tempo, but this doesn't mean the licks are easy! Here, I've taken the opportunity of the slow tempo to play some double-time lines, so as well as some 1/8 note phrases, you'll find some fast 1/16 note runs. For the faster passages, the best way to learn them is to isolate the 1/16 note phrase and play it slowly multiple times. This way, you'll commit the shape of the line to muscle memory and when you speed things up, your fingers will want to repeat the shape.

As always, try to figure out what it is that drives each phrase. Rhythmic and melodic shapes that develop throughout the line are much more important than focusing on hitting a specific target note.

Important jazz standards that contain cycles of fifths sequences with dominants chords

- *Dexterity*

- *I Got Rhythm*

- *Oleo*

- *Scrapple from the Apple*

- *Sweet Georgia Brown*

Example 5a:

Example 5b:

Example 5c:

Example 5d:

Example 5e:

Example 5f:

Example 5g:

Example 5h:

Chapter Six – Dominant Cycle of 5ths Fast

Now we're speeding up the cycle of fifths. Here it's played at a tempo similar to *Honeysuckle Rose*, which is also based on this sequence. At faster tempos, where it's not always practical (or very musical) to play streams of 1/16 notes, rhythm and phrasing are the top priority. In this collection of licks you'll also hear that I use a lot of passing notes to approach the chord tones and weave around them.

Example 6a:

Example 6b:

Example 6c:

Example 6d:

Example 6e:

Example 6f:

Example 6g:

Example 6h:

Example 6i:

Chapter Seven – D7 Static Dominant Vamp

There's a real art to sounding jazzy when there isn't a sequence of chord changes to guide your improvisation. Many soloists get stuck when faced with sixteen bars of the same chord, so understanding how to make these passages interesting is a vital tool in the box of any jazz guitarist. These dominant chords can last for whole tunes, or for just a few bars, as in a Jazz Blues. Either way, they're a great way to learn authentic jazz vocabulary without having to worry about following chord changes.

When faced with a static dominant chord for multiple bars, sometimes I'll take an approach similar to Wes Montgomery which is to *minorize* the chord. Pat Martino also plays this way, and tends to convert everything to a minor tonality.

In a nutshell, Wes or Pat would view this D7 as a V7 chord. D7 is the V7 chord in the key of G Major. With that in mind, we can imagine that we're really playing over a ii V sequence (A minor to D7) and this opens up the possibility of playing A minor scale lines or arpeggios over the D7 chord.

If you've not thought about playing this way before, this idea might seem mind-boggling to begin with, but work with it and it can really pay off. We tend to know our major and minor scales better than modes and arpeggios, and it's likely you already know more licks in A minor than you do in D Mixolydian to play over a D7 chord, so try this out in your practice times.

Superimposing a minor tonality over a dominant chord lends a cool, sophisticated sound to your jazz lines. At other times I'll mix and match ideas using D minor and major pentatonic scales to create a more bluesy sound. As before, audition all of the licks and first work on the ones that jump out at you.

Important jazz standards that contain static dominant chords

- *Almost all Jazz Blues tunes*

- *Cantaloupe Island*

- *Caravan*

- *Mercy, Mercy, Mercy*

- *Watermelon Man*

Example 7a:

Example 7b:

Example 7c:

Example 7d:

Example 7e:

Example 7f:

Example 7g:

Example 7h:

Example 7i:

Example 7j:

Example 7k:

Example 7l:

Example 7m:

Chapter Eight – ii V's Semitone Apart

This sequence consists of two ii V chords that repeat a half step apart. For example, Dm7 – G7, followed by Ebm7 – Ab7. This sequence does occasionally appear in tunes (such as John Coltrane's *Moment's Notice*) and is quite often imposed over a static chord vamp to add movement, but we're including it here for a different reason.

When soloing, you'll often come across chord sequences that are unexpected and move a little unusually. When this happens, it can be difficult to keep the natural flow of a line moving smoothly. This chapter is an exercise in tailoring vocabulary to fit the unexpected twists and turns a jazz standard might throw at you. If you can do it here, you can do it anywhere.

The challenge is to develop a vocabulary that flows smoothly over the chords, despite them moving in such a non-diatonic way. As mentioned earlier, the secret is to build lines that are based around strong rhythm and phrasing. Often the rhythm will be the driving force in a melody and have a bigger impact than the actual pitches themselves.

There's plenty of Major ii V vocabulary to learn in this chapter, so as always, audition the phrases using the audio tracks and start with the ones that most appeal. But don't lose sight of the bigger picture, which is to learn how to carry your language smoothly into slightly unexpected situations. Imagine you're a TV detective walking into a laundrette and discovering it's a front for a drugs factory!

Example 8a:

Example 8b:

Example 8c:

Example 8d:

Example 8e:

Example 8f:

Example 8g:

Example 8h:

Example 8i:

Example 8j:

Example 8k:

Example 81:

Chapter Nine – Minor 9 to Dom 13 Vamp

We're back to more common ground here with a sequence that moves from a Dm9 chord to G13. Lots of Latin Jazz tunes have this cadence, using these specific chord voicings, so it's a good one to have under your fingers. However, you can also safely ignore the G13 and treat the whole progression as a D Dorian vamp.

There are many tunes that contain long static minor 7 chord sections that require you to play Dorian solos for an extended time (such as Miles Davis' *So What* and John Coltrane's *Impressions*). Without any changes to target, many guitarists will rely solely on bluesy pentatonic vocabulary. The blues is definitely a part of the picture here and you'll certainly hear its influence in the following ideas, but using the Dorian scale really adds depth to your solo and an authentic jazz colour. (D Dorian is the second mode in the key of C Major, so D Dorian is like playing a C Major scale than begins and end on the note D).

Important jazz standards that contain static minor 7 chords

- *Chameleon*

- *Footprints*

- *Impressions*

- *Little Sunflower*

- *So What*

Example 9a:

Example 9b:

Example 9c:

Example 9d:

Example 9e:

Example 9f:

Example 9g:

Example 9h:

Example 9i:

Example 9j:

Example 9k:

Example 9l:

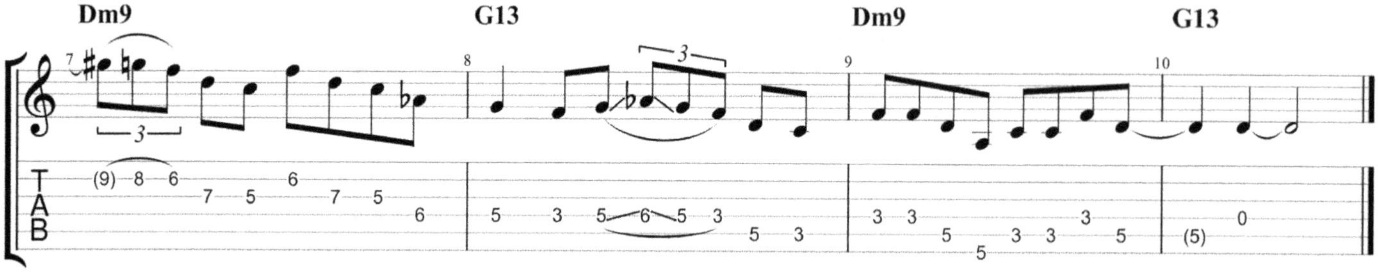
Dm9
G13
Dm9
G13

Chapter Ten – C Minor Blues

The minor blues is an essential jazz sequence that's fun to play and often there are quite a few changes added to the basic chords. The one thing that they all have in common though, is a move to the iv chord in bar five. In the key of C minor, this is a change to F minor.

The phrases in this chapter teach you some wonderful bluesy vocabulary over the first four bars and show you how to deal with the chord change in bar five. Sometimes the eight-bar phrases are split into two shorter examples to help you memorise them more easily, so make sure you learn them in conjunction with each other.

Important minor jazz blues jazz standards

- *Equinox*

- *Blue Trane*

- *Mr PC*

- *Israel*

- *Stolen Moments*

Example 10a:

Example 10b:

Example 10c:

Example 10d:

Example 10e:

Example 10f:

Chapter Eleven – Autumn Leaves: The First 8 bars Fast

In this final chapter, we're going to circle around to where we began, and revisit the changes of *Autumn Leaves*. However, this time the progression is played up tempo, so it will be more of a challenge to learn to play these phrases accurately and cleanly. You know by now that the key is to slow things down and work on small sections at a time.

In this collection of phrases you'll hear me develop some melodic/rhythmic motifs that keep things moving along and develop each idea, such as in bars 1-3 of Example 11e. You'll also hear me make use of *raked* arpeggios. This means that where the note of an arpeggio fall in a comfortable pattern on adjacent strings, we play them with a single downstroke that *pushes* through the strings. This is more efficient than trying to alternate pick them and is a life-saver at fast tempos!

Example 11a:

Example 11b:

Example 11c:

Example 11d:

Example 11e:

Example 11f:

Example 11g:

Example 11h:

Example 11i:

Melody and Variation

The phrases in this book are an excellent musical starting point that will help you develop your own unique language as a jazz guitarist, but you may be wondering where to go from here. How do you create your own solos from the melodies of jazz tunes?

It's not advanced theory that makes a fantastic player, it's developing a jazz language based around the melody of the tune. The secret is to replace the word "improvisation" with the word *variation*.

The melody is the strongest part of the tune. You don't leave a concert humming a chord progression! Almost all jazz standards were originally vocal songs, which is why they have such strong, memorable tunes. This means you can create a strong, meaningful solo by staying close to the melody and adding small variations. Even if the audience don't understand what's going on musically, they'll feel that your variations are related to the melody they've just heard. It will create a strong, tangible experience for them.

Soloing by varying the melody gives you an entire *structure* and *framework* for your solo to exist in. You'll never get "lost in the chord changes" and, most importantly, you won't have to magically create a whole new musical theme on the spot.

Very often improvisation is taught in a way that says, "You can play this scale over this chord…" but this is too far removed from what actually happens when jazz musicians start improvising. The more intuitive, melodic approach is to *vary the melody*.

Each short variation I play is what leads to the next one. Everything I play is led by my ears, but they have been trained by years of listening, copying, experimenting and playing – just like how you learned to speak.

The best way to learn this skill is to listen to great musicians playing and recycle their ideas (I always joke with my students that we're helping the planet by recycling!) These approaches are used all the time and now you know what you're listening for, it should be easier to pick them out. Even if you don't copy their idea perfectly, listening to how other musicians approach this will help you understand the melodic shapes and rhythmic possibilities you can use.

Variation can transform even the most pedestrian of melodies into a jazz solo that has momentum and tells a story. Forget about the chord changes and trust your ears. Concentrate on learning to develop your variations. The goal is to embellish the tune and build into a creative solo. Simply and gradually expand the complexity of the variations until you're playing an exciting solo. The secret is to use small variations that take the melody somewhere new. If you can do this, your audience with be right there with you. As you improve this skill, you will naturally become able to start your solos with more intricate variations and jazzier improvisations. Your only goal for now, however, is to see how many ways you can find to vary the melody.

Developing a melody depends on a few things. First of all, you can create whatever melody you like as long as it is strong and reaches the target note at the right time. Second, the more "connecting" vocabulary you have at your disposal, the more interesting your improvised lines become.

Vocabulary is learned through study and immersion in a culture – understanding how the language is constructed; its grammar and subtle nuances. You learn vocabulary through learning licks, as you've done throughout this book. You've learnt some of my jazz language by copying my playing, but as you begin to develop your own vocabulary (by using these ideas and taking them in other directions) you'll be able to use that language to speak in your own voice.

One of the dangers with the guitar is that our fingers take over when we play. We can quickly fall into playing pet licks that are part of our muscle memory and "programmed" into our body. The wonderful thing about jazz is that it is all about expressing the musical ideas we hear in our heads. Singing a line, then playing it on guitar usually results in much more melodic ideas. They are also well-formed phrases, because we need to breathe! This technique can make the biggest difference to your ability as a jazz soloist. Think of a melodic line, sing it, then play it on guitar. This is a great discipline to develop. Your lines will quickly take on a vocal quality that is missed by the majority of guitarists.

When you combine this skill with all the vocabulary you've been learning, the vocabulary will begin to influence the lines you "hear" and your jazz soloing skills will quickly compound. In fact, at this point you can really stop worrying about scales and theory, because the lines you hear, sing and play will always work!

Above all, have fun and keep developing your vocabulary.

Martin.

By the Same Author

Martin Taylor Beyond Chord Melody

• Master 7 steps to perfect jazz guitar chord melody

• Learn to create your own beautiful jazz guitar arrangements

• Discover Martin's secret approach to chord melody playing

Martin Taylor – Walking Bass for Jazz Guitar

• Learn walking baselines from the internationally acclaimed master of jazz guitar

• Discover how to effortlessly combine jazz chords and walking basslines

• Become the ultimate jazz rhythm guitar player and accompanist

Martin Taylor Single Note Soloing for Jazz Guitar

• Learn a time-honoured method for jazz improvisation that puts music before theory

• The Think, Sing, Play method that in time will lead you to be able to play any line you think of

• How to refine your jazz vocabulary and develop your phrasing

Martin Taylor's Complete Jazz Guitar Method Compilation

• Three best-selling jazz guitar books in one definitive edition:

Beyond Chord Melody

Walking Bass for Jazz Guitar

Single Note Soloing for Jazz Guitar

With almost 300 pages and hundreds of musical examples, Martin Taylor takes you on a journey through his virtuoso approaches to chord melody guitar, combining basslines with chords, and how to really solo like a jazz guitar icon.